THE HERITAGE COLLECTION

PHILIP QUAQUE

THE PIONEER SCHOOL MASTER

Letitia deGraft Okyere

Illustrated by Nouman Zafar

Lion's Historian PRESS
Amplifying Authentic Voices

Philip Quaque: The Pioneer School Master

Copyright © 2022 by Letitia deGraft Okyere

Illustrator: Nouman Zafar

Layout designer: Nasim Malik Sarkar

Library of Congress Control Number: 2022914216

All rights reserved.

No part of this publication may be reproduced, stored in a retrieval system, a database, and/or published in any form or by any means, electronic, mechanical, photocopying, recording or otherwise, without the prior written permission of the publisher.

ISBN 978-1-956776-09-6 hardback
ISBN 978-1-956776-10-2 ebook

Published by Lion's Historian Press
https://www.lionshistorian.net/

For

Sheryl Baaba and Charles Nana

CONTENTS

Chapter 1: A Cape Coast Boy 1

Chapter 2: Thompson's Student 3

Chapter 3: Living in London 5

Chapter 4: Seven Years with Rev. Moore 7

Chapter 5: Yearning for Home 9

Chapter 6: Early Teaching Days 11

Chapter 7: Establishing a Church 13

Chapter 8: Challenges with the School 15

Chapter 9: Quaque's Perseverance 17

Chapter 10: Anti-Slavery Activism 19

Epilogue: Quaque's Generational Influence 21

Glossary 23

Quiz 25

References 26

Fun Fact About the Republic of Ghana (formerly, the Gold Coast) ... 27

Author's Note 28

Other Books in the Heritage Collection 29

CHAPTER 1

A CAPE COAST BOY

Philip Quaque was born in 1741, in Cape Coast, the son of Birempong Cudjoe. Growing up among the European traders at the Cape Coast Castle, Quaque learned to read and write at an early age. Quaque was a quiet and obedient child who wanted to improve his reading and writing skills. He learned as much as he could from his teachers at the Cape Coast Castle School. Cudjoe did not fail to use his political power and influence with the Europeans to obtain additional learning opportunities for Quaque.

Cape Coast was the primary town in the Gold Coast, now modern-day Ghana, with many European traders. The traders who lived and worked at the Cape Coast Castle, where slaves were traded, worked for the British organization known as the African Company of Merchants.

CHAPTER 2

THOMPSON'S STUDENT

Quaque was about eleven years old when Cudjoe introduced him to Rev. Thomas Thompson. Quaque recognized the chance for more studies and quickly developed a relationship with Thompson. Rev. Thompson was a missionary from the Anglican Church, belonging to the SPG (or Society for the Propagation of the Gospel in Foreign Parts). Cudjoe wanted his children to receive a European-style education. He attended Rev. Thomas Thompson's first church service at the Cape Coast Castle Chapel.

Thompson opened a school away from the Cape Coast Castle for native children. Months later, he realized he would need trained teachers to keep the school running. Thompson faced the problem of which students to choose for teacher training. Before he could apply his selection plan, Cudjoe asked that Quaque be included in the list of students. Cudjoe had spoken to Quaque earlier and knew his son would not mind traveling to England.

Quaque and two other young boys, William Cudjo and Thomas Caboro, were selected by Rev. Thompson. Thompson convinced the SPG to pay for the boys' training. He argued it would be beneficial to the SPG to have trained native missionaries in the Gold Coast.

CHAPTER 3

LIVING IN LONDON

In 1754, Quaque, Caboro, and Cudjo sailed to London. The SPG placed the boys in the care of Schoolmaster Mr. Hickman in Islington. The winters were cold and the boys lonely, away from family for the first time in their lives. Quaque and his friends learned to eat different types of foods and bundle up in layers of clothing to keep warm.

Seven weeks after arrival, they were tested by the SPG's committee. The boys' results were so pleasing that the committee recommended payment to Mr. Hickman of £15 per year for each student. The students were examined again four years later, in 1758, and were found to be progressing well in their studies. Again, a pleased committee recommended to the SPG that it approve a fee increase for Mr. Hickman to £50 per year for all three boys in 1758 and £55 afterward in 1759.

Quaque's fellow student, Thomas Caboro, died in 1758 from tuberculosis after being sick for a while. Quaque and Cudjo were heartbroken, but they continued with classes, advancing to higher grades. In January 1759, Quaque and Cudjo were baptized in their adopted church at Islington.

6

CHAPTER 4

SEVEN YEARS WITH REV. MOORE

The SPG moved Quaque and Cudjo to Rev. John Moore of St. Sepulchre's Church in central London for extra studies after they were baptized. Not long after the move, Quaque was left on his own when Cudjo suffered from poor mental health and was admitted to the hospital. Cudjo never returned and died a few years later.

Quaque lived in Rev. Moore's home for seven years, taking lessons in more subjects than he did with Mr. Hickman. Quaque participated in charity work at the nearby Guy's Hospital and in religious ceremonies for inmates at the Newgate Prison.

During this time, Quaque came into close contact with members of the new group who practiced Methodism and Evangelism. Quaque joined a Black community that produced and distributed tracts describing the injustices of slavery. These experiences helped lay a foundation for Quaque's opposition to the slave trade. Later in life, Quaque would find the confidence to condemn slavery even though it was central to trading activities in the Gold Coast.

CHAPTER 5

YEARNING FOR HOME

Quaque was ordained in the Anglican Church in 1765. His teacher, Rev. Moore, reported to the SPG that Quaque showed improvement in every subject he studied. After his ordination, Quaque was ready to return home.

A few weeks after his ordination, Quaque wrote to the SPG, asking for help to resettle in Cape Coast. The SPG then appointed Quaque a missionary and schoolmaster to the people of Cape Coast, with a salary of £50 per year. Quaque would be supported by both the SPG and the African Company of Merchants.

Quaque traveled back home, arriving in February 1766. The President of the African Company of Merchants at Cape Coast gave Quaque two rooms at the Castle. Quaque immediately set to work, holding church services and teaching. Thompson's school had closed, and an excited Quaque received many requests to reopen it.

CHAPTER 6

EARLY TEACHING DAYS

Quaque first started by teaching a few students. The new President of the African Company of Merchants, Gilbert Petrie, thought this was inadequate and encouraged Quaque to take on more children. Quaque opened a school in one of his rooms for training children of British and Cape Coast traders.

Even though student numbers were small, Quaque provided instruction in religion, reading and writing, and arithmetic. Within a year of his arrival, Quaque reported students' progress in reading and religious studies to the SPG. Quaque made requests to the SPG for books while providing handwriting samples from his best students.

Within four years of Quaque's return, one of his best students was being prepared for employment as a writer at the African Company of Merchants. This trend continued with native writers finding jobs at the Cape Coast Castle and other forts in neighboring towns.

CHAPTER 7

ESTABLISHING A CHURCH

Quaque needed a large space to hold church service, so he started at his uncle's home and then moved to the *Ahenfie*, the Royal House. As a missionary, Quaque traveled outside of Cape Coast, preaching and baptizing natives. Quaque had a good friend in Anomabu, and he visited the town, about eight miles from Cape Coast. At his first Sunday service in Anomabu, Quaque preached to an enthusiastic, sizeable crowd.

However, Quaque ran into difficulties. He had problems preaching to the Europeans in Cape Coast because they did not want to listen to an African preacher. Often, European staff refused the order of the President of the African Company of Merchants to attend Sunday Service, and services were canceled. The Cape Coast Castle garrison made fun of Quaque's preaching efforts.

In addition, Quaque had lost his ability to speak his native language, Fante, and was forced to preach to his fellow people through an interpreter. This made his work as a preacher to the natives very difficult. Many did not appreciate the fact that he was unable to speak Fante after only a few years in England. Close to ten years after his return, Quaque had only baptized fifty-two persons, primarily Europeans. Quaque had similar struggles when he moved seventy miles away to Dixcove for eight months.

CHAPTER 8

CHALLENGES WITH THE SCHOOL

Quaque's struggles extended to maintaining the school. He asked the SPG to help with a school building so he could increase teachers and students. Quaque added a request for school supplies. Both requests were ignored by the SPG and the African Company of Merchants in London, who had responsibility for the school's upkeep. The President of the African Company of Merchants in Cape Coast made conditions worse when he took away one of Quaque's rooms to house sick soldiers, leaving Quaque with just one room, where he lived and held classes.

To help raise funds, Quaque established a local education authority within the new Freemason movement called the *Torridzonian* Society. The Society held weekly social events with expenses met through mandatory contributions. This was successful, and Quaque used these extra funds to establish a school.

The school flourished, and Quaque reported in 1791 to the SPG that the children of the Torridzonians made good progress. Unfortunately, a disagreement arose among the Society's leaders, and it had a negative effect on the school. However, Quaque did not give up; he continually wrote to the SPG for assistance. In 1795, Quaque, still intent on reviving the school, sent writing specimens from three of his best students, hoping to convince the SPG to send him essential supplies.

CHAPTER 9

QUAQUE'S PERSEVERANCE

Quaque devised methods to keep the school open when the SPG repeatedly ignored requests for assistance and failed to make timely salary payments. He took up trading for food, clothing, and other necessities, leading to his indebtedness to other traders. Quaque must have been close to starvation at times because at his death, it was revealed that the SPG owed him £369 in unpaid salary.

In 1791, the Governor at Anomabu ordered Quaque to help defend the fort. He refused because it went against his Christian beliefs. Quaque was suspended by the African Company of Merchant's officials in Cape Coast and Anomabu and evicted from his lodgings at the Cape Coast Castle. Quaque rented accommodation in the town and then appealed to the African Company of Merchants in London. Quaque's position as chaplain was reinstated, and he received a pay increase.

Quaque had other troubles. As medical science was not advanced, there were many diseases that affected life in Cape Coast, leading to deaths. Quaque lost family members. There were threats of war from an inland group, the Ashanti, against Cape Coast and other coastal towns. Disagreements between Cape Coast natives and European traders led to open conflicts. In 1803, during a dispute between the people of Cape Coast and European traders, the Governor of the Cape Coast Castle fired the castle guns and destroyed the town.

Despite these problems that made the running of a church and school a challenge for Quaque, he was respected in Cape Coast. When the need arose, Quaque's signature was added to agreements between Europeans and natives to secure peace in Cape Coast.

CHAPTER 10

ANTI-SLAVERY ACTIVISM

After Quaque returned to the Gold Coast, he did not forget the anti-slavery connections he had made in England. Quaque first started by expressing his dislike of slavery in private letters to abolitionists like Samuel Hopkins and the slave girl turned poet Phillis Wheatley in America. Quaque explained that slavery interfered with his missionary work in Cape Coast. However, as the SPG and African Company of Merchants depended on each other in the slave trade, these private letters, if made public, could have cost Quaque his job.

As the abolitionist movement grew, Quaque showed more courage with public letters. Quaque wrote to the SPG, discussing the evil slave trade and its negative impact on the coast. Quaque went further with a condemnation of slavery to the SPG when slaves revolted on a Dutch ship docked at the Gold Coast. Quaque informed his employers that the wicked treatment by the ship's captain caused the revolt where many slaves on board died.

Quaque later provided slavery abolitionists in Britain with information on the cruelties of the slave trade. When abolitionists such as Alexander Falconbridge and Lieutenant John Simpson testified before the British Parliament, they relied on critical information provided by Quaque. Quaque's evidence indicated that slaves were cruelly kidnapped and that the practice increased violence in the Gold Coast. Quaque gave visiting abolitionists evidence of cultural and physical damage caused by slave trading in Cape Coast. Britain finally abolished slavery with an Act of Parliament in 1807.

EPILOGUE

QUAQUE'S GENERATIONAL INFLUENCE

Quaque remained a dedicated missionary until his death in 1816 at the age of seventy-five years. For fifty years, Quaque attempted to establish an Anglican Church mission in the Gold Coast. He toiled under difficult conditions amidst the horrors of the slave trade and racism. The Europeans traders that Quaque served as chaplain made fun of his efforts. His fellow natives grew impatient with him because he lost the ability to speak Fante and of his links to slave trading at the Castle. Yet, as the first African missionary to the Gold Coast, his efforts produced teachers who took his legacy into the next century and beyond.

Rev. Philip Quaque laid the foundation for European-style education in the nation. He opened the door for Basel missionaries who established industrial training for the youth in the eastern part of the country. Quaque's students formed the Bible Band, providing the Gold Coast Methodist Church with founding members. Quaque laid the groundwork for Wesleyan missionaries who founded the country's first boys' secondary school, Mfantsipim, and many other institutions, including the Wesley Girls' High School.

Though Quaque's life was not one of abundant victories, it was a story of dedication and perseverance, earning him the place of Gold Coast's (or Ghana's) pioneering educator. Quaque's success rested on two tenets. First, on his native pupils. These pupils were the first generation of European style educated Africans who set the pace for social, economic, and political change in the country. Second, on his contribution to the abolition of slavery by the British Parliament. The African Company of Merchants honored Quaque with a memorial at the Cape Coast Castle, which still exists today.

GLOSSARY

Birempong — An informal title, indicating a person of influence and wealth.

Company of Merchants — The Company of Merchants, also the African Company of Merchants, was a British company operating around the Gold Coast. It participated in the slave trade.

The Anglican Church — Also known as the Church of England, it is one of the largest branches of Christianity, and its members are called Anglicans.

SPG — The SPG, or Society for the Propagation of the Gospel in Foreign Parts, was the missionary branch of the Church of England.

Rev. Thomas Thompson — Thomas Thompson, a graduate of Cambridge University, was the first Anglican Church missionary to the Gold Coast, now Ghana.

Islington — Islington is a district in central London.

Guy's Hospital — Guy's Hospital is a large teaching hospital in London founded in 1721.

Newgate Prison   This was a prison in central London built in the 1300s. It was closed in 1902, and the famous criminal court called Old Bailey occupies much of the premises.

Ahenfie   The Royal House where the king lives and holds court.

Torridzonian Society   This was a Freemason group established in Cape Coast.

Fante   This is the language spoken by the people of Cape Coast.

Abolitionists   A person who wants to end a practice, in this case, the slave trade.

QUIZ

1. Where was Philip Quaque born?

    (a) Dixcove
    (b) Anomabu
    (c) Cape Coast
    (d) Elmina

2. Who was Philip Quaque's first European teacher?

    (a) Rev. Thomas Thompson
    (b) Mr. Hickman
    (c) Mr. Moore
    (d) Phillis Wheatley

3. Why was Quaque suspended by the Company of Merchants and evicted from his lodgings at the Cape Coast Castle?

    (a) Because he preached to the European traders
    (b) Because he started trading to earn extra money
    (c) Because he refused to teach
    (d) Because he refused to fight to defend the Anomabu fort

4. When did Philip Quaque die?

    (a) 1758
    (b) 1816
    (c) 1805
    (d) 1796

QUIZ ANSWERS: CADB

REFERENCES

Carretta, Vincent. *Phillis Wheatley: Biography of a Genius in Bondage*. Athens, University of Georgia Press, 2011.

Glasson, Travis. "Missionaries, Methodists, and a Ghost: Philip Quaque in London and Cape Coast, 1756-1816." *Journal of British Studies*, vol. 48, no. 1, January 2009, pp. 29-50.

Casely-Hayford, Augustus. *Genealogical History of Cape Coast Stool Families*. Ph.D. Dissertation, University of London School of Oriental and African Studies, 1992.

Bansa, Grace. "Quaque, P." *Encyclopedia Africana Dictionary of African Biography, Volume 1, Ethiopia – Ghana*, edited by L.H. Ofosu-Appiah, Reference Publications Inc., 1977, pp. 305-306.

Sampson, Magnus. *Makers of Modern Ghana*. Accra, Anowuo Educational Publications, 1969.

Bartels, Francis L. "Philip Quaque, 1741-1816." *Transactions of the Gold Coast and Togoland Historical Society*, vol. 1, no. 5, 1955, pp. 153-177.

FUN FACT ABOUT THE REPUBLIC OF GHANA (FORMERLY, THE GOLD COAST)

The national cloth or costume is called kente. It is made from long strips of fabric sown together to make the finished cloth. Weavers use wooden handlooms to create the long strips from colorful silk or cotton yarns. Kente fabrics vary in patterns, many of which have names or convey a message. Kente is said to have been developed by weavers who wanted to copy how spiders weave webs.

AUTHOR'S NOTE

Through the Heritage Collection's historical biographies for children, the author endeavors to tell the stories of men and women of African descent who changed the course of events within their circles of influence.

Historical biographies are important for child development. When a child can see him- or herself represented in the life of people who grew up to effect social, economic, or political change, he or she is more likely to be inspired to meet and overcome life's challenges.

Thus, the author's purpose is simple: to enable children to fulfill their destinies by seeing themselves through others who rose above difficulties to bring about change.

OTHER BOOKS IN THE HERITAGE COLLECTION

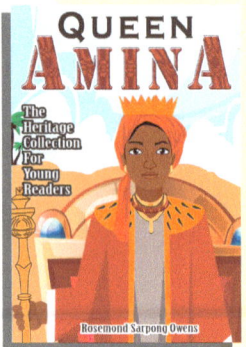

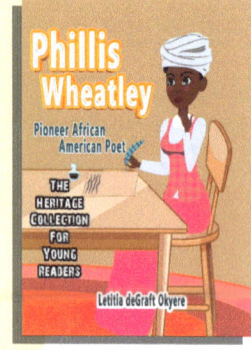
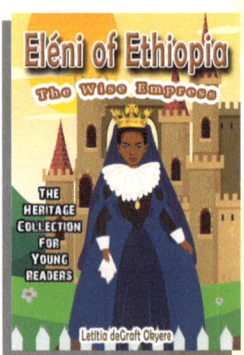
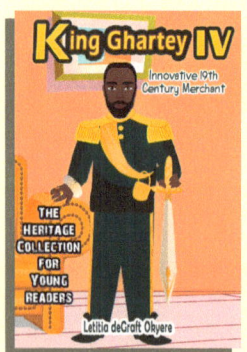
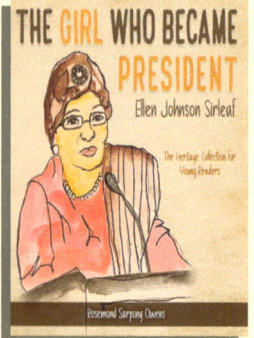
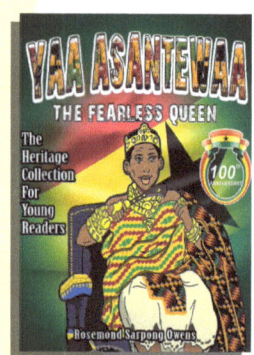
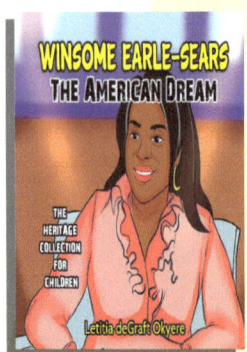
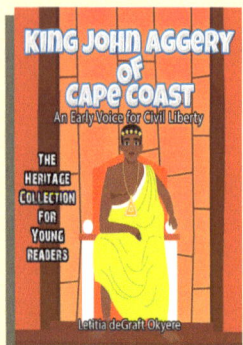

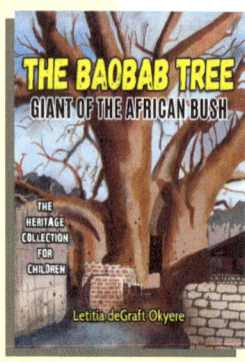

www.ingramcontent.com/pod-product-compliance
Lightning Source LLC
Chambersburg PA
CBHW041405010526
44107CB00015B/1083